YAKALOU MEDIA

ARE YOU READY TO COMING OUT?

Let's Find Out With These 100 Thought Provoking Yes Or No Questions

First edition

This book was professionally typeset on Reedsy.
Find out more at reedsy.com

Contents

Disclaimer

This book is designed to provide information only. This information is provided and sold with the knowledge that the publisher and author do not offer any legal or other professional advice. In the case of a need for any such expertise, consult with the appropriate professional.

This book does not contain all the information available on the subject. This book has not been created to be specific to any individual's or organization's situation or needs. Every effort has been made to make this book as accurate as possible. However, there may be typographical and/or content errors. Therefore, this book should serve only as a general guide, not as the ultimate source of subject information.

This book contains information that might be dated and is intended only to educate and entertain. Regarding any loss or damage allegedly suffered or alleged to have occurred as a result of the information in this book, either directly or indirectly, the author and publisher shall have no liability or responsibility to any person or entity.

I

Before Diving Deep

Introdution

Have you ever felt like you're standing on the edge of a diving board, gazing into the pool below, but uncertain if you're ready to make the leap? That heart-pounding feeling of anticipation, combined with a flurry of questions: Is the water too cold? What if I don't dive right? Will people watch and judge? Now, imagine if that pool was your life, and the dive represented revealing your true self to the world. Quite a dive, isn't it?

Coming out isn't just about uttering the words; it's a deeply personal journey, filled with ups and downs. You might be asking yourself: Will my friends understand? How will my family react? Is the world ready to embrace the real me? And perhaps the most significant question of them all: Am I ready?

This book is your companion for answering these questions and many more. Think of it as a mirror, reflecting your thoughts, feelings, and apprehensions. On every page, we'll delve into the facets of your life, from the most intimate recesses of self-acceptance to the broader perspectives of public perception.

So, are you curious? Ready to embark on a journey of introspection and discovery? Because by the end of these 100 yes-or-no questions, you might just find the clarity you've been seeking. And who knows? Maybe you'll be ready to take that dive, with confidence, grace, and, most importantly, self-assurance.

The "Yes or No Questions Concept"

Do you remember playing '20 Questions' as a kid? That thrilling game where every answer brought you closer to uncovering the secret? Well, isn't life a bit like that—a series of questions guiding us toward deeper understanding? But here's a twist: What if you only had two options to answer those life questions: "Yes" or "No"? Sounds simple, doesn't it? Or does it?

In our busy lives, we're often swamped with a million shades of maybe, perhaps, and possibly. But what if we stripped away the ambiguity? Dropped the clutter? Just for a moment, imagine the clarity that could come from decisive answers. The "Yes or No Questions Concept" challenges you to do just that. It's about confronting the core, confronting the truth, and confronting ourselves.

You might wonder: Can a straightforward "yes" or "no" truly encapsulate our complex feelings and situations? The beauty of this approach lies in its simplicity. It forces us to confront, make a choice, and acknowledge our genuine feelings. While it might seem like a binary approach, the real magic unfolds in the spaces between these answers—the introspection, the moments of pause, and the revelations.

So, are you intrigued? Eager to delve into this realm of black and white, discovering the vibrant spectrum of emotions it unveils? Dive in, challenge yourself, and embrace the beauty of clarity and self-awareness. Because, sometimes, the simplest questions lead us to the most profound realizations.

The Rules of the "Yes or No Questions" Game

Do you recall the thrill of opening a new board game and eagerly flipping through the rulebook before diving into play? No matter how simple, every game has guidelines to ensure clarity and fairness. So, before we journey through the maze of "Yes or No questions", what say we set down some ground rules?

First off, think about this: What's the essence of a game? Fun, right? And perhaps a touch of challenge. That's precisely what we're aiming for. The key to the "Yes or No Questions" game concept is to be authentic, raw, and true. But how can you ensure that your answers aren't swayed by what you think you 'should' say? Or what others might want to hear?

- **Rule Number One:**

Listen to Your Gut. When a question pops up, take a deep breath and let your immediate gut reaction guide your response. You might be surprised at how wise your first instinct can be!

- **Rule Number Two:**

No Overthinking Allowed. It's easy to get lost in the 'what ifs' and the whirlwind of potential scenarios. But remember, this is a game of instinct, not analysis. Answer from the heart, not the head.

· **And lastly, Rule Number Three:**

No Judgments. This is a safe space, a judgment-free zone. Whether you're exploring these questions alone or sharing them with others, remember that every "yes" or "no" is valid. Your feelings, your experiences, and your answers are uniquely yours.

Now that we've laid out the rules, are you feeling a tingle of anticipation? An itch to start? Dive in with an open mind and heart, and let's uncover the wonders that lie in the simple words "yes" and "no". Because, in this game, the real prize is the journey of self-discovery.

How to Interpret the Result

Remember those quizzes in magazines where, after ticking off boxes and tallying up scores, you'd eagerly flip to the back page to see what the results revealed about you? Well, think of this chapter as that revealing back page. But here's the catch: instead of telling you which celebrity you're most like, these results will illuminate facets of your inner self.

First things first: Does the number of "yes" or "no" answers determine whether you're right or wrong? The simple answer? Absolutely not. This isn't a test with a passing or failing grade. It's more like a compass, guiding you through your feelings, beliefs, and aspirations.

So, what does a majority of "yes" answers imply? And what if you find yourself leaning more toward "no"? The beauty of this interpretation isn't in the count but in the introspection. However, to give some structure to your journey, here's a brief guide:

- **Majority of "Yes" Answers:** Perhaps you're someone who resonates with affirmation, positivity, or agreement with the contexts provided. This might indicate readiness, acceptance, or a forward-leaning perspective. But, and here's the question, is it always because you genuinely feel that way?

- **Majority of "No" Answers:** This might suggest that you

have reservations, concerns, or differing experiences from the scenarios posed. It could hint at caution, a need for more information, or simply a different path. Again, the crux lies in asking, is this an authentic reflection of my feelings?

However, here's the golden rule of interpretation: Your Answers Are Your Own. No one, not even this book, can tell you how to feel or what your answers signify for sure. The real value lies in the moments of reflection these results spark.

So, as you sift through your tally, are you ready to dive deeper into what these "yes" or "no" responses reveal? Ready to embrace the clarity, accept the uncertainties, and cherish the journey of self-awareness? After all, the quest for understanding oneself is the most intriguing journey of all.

II

Your 100 Thought-Provoking "Yes or No" Questions

Chapter 1: Self-Acceptance

Coming out to the world starts with coming out to oneself. Self-acceptance isn't just the beginning of our journey; it's the foundation upon which everything else stands. Before we can share our truth with others, we must first be honest and gentle with ourselves. Recognizing and loving who we truly are might seem simple on paper, but it's an intricate dance of understanding, embracing, and celebrating our authentic selves.

Choosing "Self-Acceptance" as the first chapter is intentional. We often rush to think about how others will perceive us, pushing our personal feelings aside. But this chapter flips that perspective. Before we can step out and share our truth with the world, it's crucial to reflect inward. By starting here, we're affirming a simple but powerful fact: your journey begins with YOU. It's not about seeking external validation, but about acknowledging and fostering self-worth.

The process of self-acceptance can be transformative. Embracing who you are eliminates the weight of pretending and offers a clarity that's both liberating and grounding. Whether you're feeling certain or lost, strong or vulnerable, understanding and accepting your own feelings and identity is a compass that will guide you, even when the path gets rough.

As you navigate this chapter, remember: it's okay to be

uncertain. This is your journey, and there's no deadline for understanding yourself. It's perfectly alright to sit with your feelings, to question them, and to take the time you need. The questions at the end of this chapter are designed to help you take the first steps toward that understanding. They aren't about right or wrong, but they are tools for introspection.

To truly grasp where you stand on the road to coming out, start by understanding and acknowledging your feelings. Here are ten straightforward questions to guide you. Answer them honestly, remembering there's no judgment here, only growth.

1. Have you accepted your own sexuality or gender identity?
2. Do you feel proud of who you are?
3. Do you often wish you were "normal" or like everyone else?
4. Have you ever tried to change who you are because of external pressures?
5. Do you believe you deserve happiness and love just as you are?
6. Are there days when you feel confused about your feelings?
7. Do you hide your true self even when you're alone?
8. Are you afraid of what self-acceptance means for your future?
9. Have you educated yourself about your own feelings and identity?
10. Do you feel guilt or shame about your true self?

Take your time with these questions. Reflect on them, ponder them, and use them as a mirror to truly see and understand yourself. Remember, the journey to coming out begins with a single step, and that step is self-acceptance.

Chapter 2: Safety and Environment

Imagine you're a budding plant. You need the right conditions to grow and thrive: nourishing soil, ample sunlight, and protective surroundings. Just like this plant, your journey of coming out requires a safe and supportive environment. It's important to ensure you're in a physical and emotional space that allows you to grow into your true self without unnecessary harm.

Why begin with "Safety and Environment"? Because before we can address anything else—our feelings, our relationships, our dreams—we must first establish our basic well-being. Coming out can be an empowering act, but it can also carry risks, especially in less accepting environments. By focusing on safety first, we emphasize the importance of your well-being and recognize that every individual's situation is unique.

Understanding your surroundings and recognizing potential challenges is crucial. It's not about instilling fear, but rather being prepared. Knowledge equips you, and with the right knowledge, you can make informed decisions. It's about knowing when to speak, when to stay silent, and when to find a new environment that offers you the warmth and acceptance you deserve.

The questions that follow are designed to help you reflect on your environment. They will encourage you to think about your community, your home, and your day-to-day surroundings, and whether they're conducive to your safety and well-being. Remember, this isn't a race. It's your personal journey, and it's essential to ensure your path is as smooth and safe as possible.

Let's delve deeper into understanding your environment. Consider the following questions and answer them with the utmost honesty:

1. Do you live in a community where being LGBTQ+ is generally accepted?
2. Have you heard negative remarks about LGBTQ+ people in your surroundings?
3. Do you feel safe expressing yourself in your current environment?
4. Are there local resources or places where you feel supported?
5. Are you aware of any local laws or regulations related to LGBTQ+ rights?
6. Do you know someone personally who has faced backlash for coming out?
7. Would you feel endangered if someone disclosed your sexuality or gender identity without your permission?
8. Is there a chance your housing situation might be jeopardized by coming out?
9. Do local authorities and institutions support and protect LGBTQ+ rights?
10. Have you considered relocating for safety and acceptance reasons?

As you reflect on these questions, let them guide you not just in your decision to come out, but also in understanding how to navigate your environment afterward. Remember, your safety and well-being are paramount. Every flower deserves the right to bloom in its own time, and in its own space. Let's ensure you find yours.

Chapter 3: Family Relations

The saying goes, "Blood is thicker than water." For many, family is the cornerstone of their existence, the backdrop of their life story, and the ever-present safety net. But for someone within the LGBTQ+ spectrum, the idea of family can be both a haven and a source of apprehension. The thought of coming out to those we've grown up with, who've known us since our first steps, can be daunting. This chapter, "Family Relations," dives deep into these complex dynamics to help you navigate the most intimate relationships in your life.

Choosing "Family Relations" as a chapter is essential because families often play a significant role in how we view ourselves and our place in the world. The acceptance, or lack thereof, from our family can profoundly impact our emotional well-being. But it's essential to remember that family isn't just about biology. It's about love, understanding, and shared experiences. Whether it's the family we're born into or the one we choose, these relationships mold our sense of self-worth and belonging.

Approaching the subject of "coming out" with family is unique. Unlike friends or acquaintances, family bonds come with years of shared memories, understanding, and at times, expectations. You might be grappling with concerns about disappointing loved ones, altering family dynamics, or changing the way your family sees you. But through all these worries, it's crucial to remember that true family bonds are built on love and understanding, and they can weather many storms.

The following questions aim to make you reflect on your family's dynamics, their beliefs, and how they might impact your decision to come out. They're designed to provide clarity and maybe even highlight areas where you feel supported or concerned. As you ponder these questions, remember that every family is different. Use these as a guide, not a blueprint.

Reflect on the following with utmost sincerity:

1. Have family members expressed supportive views about LGBTQ+ topics in the past?
2. Have you heard your family make derogatory remarks about LGBTQ+ individuals?
3. Do you think your family's cultural or religious beliefs might impact their response?
4. Do you feel your family relies heavily on traditional gender roles?
5. Are there other family members who have come out?
6. Do you worry that your family will treat you differently after coming out?
7. Do family gatherings make you feel particularly anxious?
8. Are there family members you're especially nervous about telling?
9. Do you feel you might be at risk of physical or emotional harm within your family?
10. Is there a chance of financial cut-off from family after coming out?
11. Is there a family member you believe might be particularly supportive? Who? List them?

12. Do you worry about being isolated or ostracized by your family?
13. Do you feel the need to protect your siblings or younger family members from the truth?

Family relations can be both a source of strength and anxiety when considering coming out. As you venture deeper into understanding your family dynamics, remember to prioritize your well-being and mental health. Sometimes, the journey toward acceptance starts with just one understanding family member. And other times, it may mean seeking support outside the familial fold. Whichever path you tread, know that your chosen family awaits, ready to embrace you with open arms.

Chapter 4: Friendships

In the tapestry of life, friends are those vibrant threads that add color, texture, and beauty. They're our partners in crime during our rebellious phases, our shoulders to cry on during the hard times, and our biggest cheerleaders as we chase our dreams. For many, friends become an extended family, a tribe with whom we share our deepest secrets and our most unfiltered selves. It's precisely this closeness and sincerity that makes the thought of coming out to friends a mix of anticipation and anxiety. This chapter, "Friendships," seeks to guide you through this intricate dance of vulnerability and trust.

Why focus on "Friendships"? Because for many, our circle of friends is where we first experiment with self-expression. They see versions of us that even family might not be privy to. Friends bear witness to our growth, our changes, and our evolutions. Yet, there's often a lurking fear: What if coming out changes the dynamics of these cherished relationships? This chapter aims to help you navigate these waters with sensitivity and confidence.

Friends, unlike family, are the relationships we choose. They're based on mutual likes, shared experiences, and an understanding that often feels telepathic. The beauty of friendships lies in their flexibility and capacity for growth. Whether it's the childhood buddy who's seen you through braces and bad haircuts or the college mate who became an unexpected soulmate, every friend relationship has its rhythm. Understanding this rhythm can guide you on how, when, and where to have the conversation about your true self.

The following questions have been crafted to encourage introspection about your friendships. They will guide you to gauge the temperature of these relationships and provide insights into how your truth might be received. Remember, friendships, like all relationships, ebb and flow. These questions will help you find the right tide to ride.

Reflect deeply on the following:

1. Do you believe your closest friends will support you?
2. Are there specific friends you're apprehensive about telling?
3. Have you ever felt the need to hide or alter aspects of yourself within your friend circle?
4. Are you worried about changing dynamics in same-gender friendships after coming out?
5. Do you have friends who are openly LGBTQ+?
6. Are you scared of being the subject of gossip or rumors?
7. Have any friends questioned or speculated about your sexuality or gender identity before?
8. Are there friends you've considered distancing yourself from due to their views?
9. Do you feel that your friendships are based on mutual trust and understanding?
10. Are you part of groups or clubs that might not be accepting?
11. Would you consider seeking new friendships in LGBTQ+ inclusive spaces?

Navigating friendships while revealing your true self can be a delicate journey, but it provides opportunities for deeper connections and stronger bonds. Remember, true friends embrace you for who you are, and those who matter won't mind. And if they do, maybe it's time to question if they truly belong in the chapter of your life titled "Friendships."

Chapter 5: Work and School

In the theater of life, work and school are stages where we often play multiple roles. From being a diligent student or a dedicated employee to forging relationships with peers and mentors, these are spaces where we spend significant chunks of our lives. They shape our worldviews, challenge our beliefs, and often help carve our identities. Yet, they are also environments defined by their own sets of rules, expectations, and social dynamics. This chapter, "Work and School," explores these structured realms and guides you in navigating your coming out journey within them.

Why spotlight "Work and School"? While personal relationships have their complexities, institutional and professional settings come with an additional layer of intricacies. There's the need to maintain a certain decorum, the pressure to conform to often unspoken norms, and the constant dance between personal authenticity and professional appropriateness. Balancing being true to oneself while navigating these spaces can be challenging, making it crucial to approach the topic with care and foresight.

School is where young minds blossom. It's where friendships are forged, opinions are formed, and identities are discovered. It's also a place where peer pressure is tangible, and the need for acceptance can sometimes overshadow the importance of self-acceptance. Similarly, the workplace, with its hierarchies and power dynamics, can be a minefield for anyone contemplating coming out. It's not just about colleagues; it's about bosses, subordinates, clients, and the organization's overarching culture.

The subsequent questions are curated to prompt reflection about your specific situation in work or school. They're tailored to make you think about the environment, the people, and the potential repercussions, both positive and negative. As you contemplate these, remember that every institution and organization is different, and what applies in one may not in another.

Ponder deeply on the following:

1. Does your school or workplace have a known policy supporting LGBTQ+ rights?
2. Have you witnessed or heard of discrimination based on sexual orientation or gender identity in these settings?
3. Are there support groups, clubs, or allies within your school or workplace that cater to LGBTQ+ individuals?
4. Do you feel your academic or professional growth might be impacted by coming out?
5. Have you encountered peers, teachers, or colleagues who openly identify as LGBTQ+?
6. Do you feel comfortable discussing personal matters with superiors or teachers?
7. Do you believe your relationships with peers or colleagues will change after coming out?
8. Is there a trusted mentor, teacher, or senior at work or school whom you feel safe confiding in?

9. Is there a risk of losing opportunities or scholarships by coming out?
10. Would you consider transferring jobs or schools if reactions were negative?

Work and school are not just about learning subjects or skills, but about learning life. As you stand at the intersection of personal authenticity and external expectations, remember that while it's essential to be true to oneself, it's equally crucial to ensure that this revelation doesn't compromise your safety or well-being. Here's to finding that balance and scripting a narrative that's as empowering as it is true.

Chapter 6: Emotional Readiness*

Our emotions are like the vast, boundless ocean: sometimes calm, sometimes stormy, but always deep and ever-present. They guide our decisions, influence our actions, and shape our interactions. As we stand on the precipice of coming out, emotional readiness becomes the anchor that grounds us. It's the internal compass that helps us navigate the waves of acceptance, rejection, joy, and fear. This chapter, "Emotional Readiness," delves into the depths of our hearts and minds, exploring the myriad feelings associated with revealing our true selves.

Why zone in on "Emotional Readiness"? Because coming out isn't just an external act of telling the world who you are; it's an internal journey of accepting oneself with all its vulnerabilities and strengths. The external environment, be it family, friends, work, or school, plays its part, but the heart of the matter lies within. Are you emotionally equipped to handle the range of reactions, both positive and negative? Do you have the internal resilience to stay true to yourself, even when faced with adversity?

Emotions are complex. On one hand, there's the euphoria of unburdening a secret and the lightness of being authentic. On the other hand, there's the trepidation of unforeseen reactions and the fear of the unknown. Emotional readiness isn't about suppressing negative feelings but understanding and acknowledging them. It's about ensuring you're mentally and emotionally equipped to handle the rollercoaster of responses and consequences that might follow.

The ensuing questions are formulated to guide you through your emotional landscape. They will prompt introspection, help you identify areas of strength, and highlight spaces where you might need support. As you ponder these questions, remember to be gentle with yourself; emotional readiness is a journey, not a destination.

Dive deep into your feelings and consider the following:

1. Do you feel at peace with your own understanding and acceptance of your sexuality or gender identity?
2. Have you processed potential scenarios, both positive and negative, post coming out?
3. Do you have a support system in place, be it friends, family, or professionals, for post-disclosure emotions?
4. Are there unresolved feelings or past experiences that might amplify your current emotions?
5. Do you feel pressured, either internally or externally, to come out before you're emotionally ready?
6. Have you considered seeking professional counseling or therapy to navigate your feelings?
7. Are you prepared to face potential negative reactions without it affecting your self-worth?
8. Do moments of doubt overshadow your moments of clarity when thinking about coming out?
9. Are you confident in your ability to seek help or communicate when feeling overwhelmed?

10. Have you recognized and celebrated the strength and courage inherent in your journey so far?

Emotional readiness is like the foundation of a house: it supports and sustains the structure above. As you prepare to step into your truth, ensure that your foundation is solid. Embrace the beauty of your emotions, for they are the raw, authentic essence of who you are. And as you tread this path, remember that it's okay to seek help, lean on others, and take your time. Your emotional well-being is paramount.

Chapter 7: Public Perception

We live in a world where the personal often intertwines with the public. From the opinions of neighbors and acquaintances to the more expansive realm of social media followers and online communities, public perception holds a magnifying glass to our lives. This chapter, "Public Perception," shines a light on the broader societal view, the collective mindset, and how it can impact our personal narrative of coming out.

Why dissect "Public Perception"? While the act of coming out is deeply personal, its ramifications often extend into the public sphere. Our stories can spread, affecting people we've never met and influencing opinions we're unaware of in an era where digital connections and virtual networks are prevalent. While it's vital not to let public opinion dictate our personal truth, it's equally important to understand its potential impact and be prepared for it.

Public perception is a kaleidoscope, continually shifting and changing. One day it might be supportive, the next indifferent, and sometimes, unfortunately, hostile. The broader society's views on LGBTQ+ issues have evolved considerably over the years, but there still exist pockets of prejudice and misunderstanding. Navigating this terrain requires a blend of courage, tact, and, sometimes, a thick skin.

The questions below are designed to make you contemplate the broader public's potential reactions and your place within that larger context. They are prompts to make you consider both the warmth of communal support and the potential chill of societal judgment.

Reflect on the following:

1. Are you comfortable being perceived as an LGBTQ+ individual in public spaces?
2. Do you worry about public displays of affection being judged?
3. Are you okay with possibly becoming an advocate or role model by default?
4. Do you fear public backlash on social media?
5. Are you concerned about your safety in public after coming out?
6. Would you be willing to join public LGBTQ+ events or parades?
7. Are you comfortable with possible attention or curiosity from strangers?
8. Do you feel the need to represent or fit into LGBTQ+ stereotypes?
9. Are you okay with people asking personal or invasive questions?
10. Would you consider changing daily routines or habits due to public perception?

The court of public opinion is vast and varied. While it's essential to be aware of its potential influence, it's crucial to remember that your journey is your own. It's about your truth, your narrative, and your happiness. As you navigate the balance between the personal and public, may you find strength in authenticity and solace in the knowledge that every act of coming out, big or small, contributes to a broader understanding and acceptance in society.

Chapter 8: Relationships and Dating

Love, a universal emotion, is as exhilarating as it is complex. In the dance of attraction, connection, and companionship, we often find reflections of our true selves. Relationships and dating form the backdrop against which many of our personal stories unfold, offering both joys and challenges. This chapter, "Relationships and Dating," peers into the romantic facet of our lives, exploring how coming out might interplay with our pursuits of the heart.

Why delve into "Relationships and Dating"? Because coming out isn't an isolated event; it's intrinsically tied to how we connect emotionally and romantically with others. Understanding one's sexuality or gender identity often correlates with how one experiences and expresses love. Thus, coming out can be a crucial cornerstone in forming genuine, fulfilling relationships and navigating the dating world with authenticity.

The landscape of love is ever-evolving. From the initial butterflies of a crush to the profound bond of a long-term relationship, each stage presents its nuances. Add to this the dynamics of coming out, and you have a tapestry rich in emotion, introspection, and growth. For some, coming out might mean redefining existing relationships; for others, it could signify a fresh start.

The questions that follow are aimed at helping you explore this intersection of love, identity, and revelation. They are meant to prompt introspection about past relationships, current connections, and future aspirations in romance.

Consider the following as you navigate your heart's journey:

1. Are you ready to pursue relationships that align with your true self?
2. Do you feel the need to come out to past romantic partners?
3. Are you worried about the perception of your current romantic relationship?
4. Do you feel comfortable navigating the dating world as an openly LGBTQ+ individual?
5. Are you worried about the challenges of dating within the LGBTQ+ community?
6. Do you feel you have to conform to certain roles in relationships?
7. Are you okay with friends or family knowing about your LGBTQ+ relationships?
8. Do you know where to find resources or information on LGBTQ+ dating?
9. Are you concerned about potential discrimination in the dating scene?
10. Are you ready to address potential relationship challenges due to coming out?

Relationships and dating, in essence, are about finding someone who resonates with your soul, someone who celebrates your authentic self. As you stand at the juncture of self-revelation and romantic connections, remember that love, in its purest form, seeks understanding, acceptance, and authenticity. May your journey to coming out be a bridge to deeper, more genuine connections, painting your life with the vibrant colors of love.

35

Chapter 9: Future Planning

As humans, we have an innate desire to look forward, to envision a tomorrow that reflects our aspirations, dreams, and values. This very act of forward-thinking, of crafting a vision for ourselves, plays an integral role in how we shape our present actions. This chapter, titled "Future Planning," beckons you to reflect upon the horizon, considering how your coming out journey aligns with the life you envisage for yourself.

Why emphasize "Future Planning"? Because coming out is not merely a present moment declaration; it's a fundamental part of who you will be in the days, months, and years to come. Understanding and revealing your true self can deeply influence major life decisions, from career paths to starting a family, to determining where you'd like to reside. It's a thread that, knowingly or unknowingly, might weave through various aspects of your future.

Life's path is seldom linear. It's filled with crossroads, detours, and uncharted territories. The act of coming out can sometimes feel like standing at one such crossroad, gazing into the potential paths ahead. For some, the path may be clear, while for others, it might still be forming.

The questions below are framed to help you project into the future, looking at various facets of life and how your authentic self fits into those plans. They're prompts designed to meld your present state of being with your aspirations for the future. Ponder on the following as you look ahead:

1. Do you see your true self in your future plans?
2. Are you worried about potential challenges in family planning or adoption?
3. Do you consider LGBTQ+ rights when thinking of places to live in the future?
4. Are you concerned about potential health or medical challenges related to being LGBTQ+?
5. Do you feel the need to adjust life milestones based on coming out?
6. Are you comfortable potentially being an LGBTQ+ parent?
7. Do you worry about how society might change in terms of LGBTQ+ acceptance?
8. Do you feel the need to prioritize safety over personal desires in the future?
9. Do you see yourself as a part of the broader LGBTQ+ community in the future?
10. Are there life goals you feel might be compromised by coming out?
11. Have you set aside moments to dream, visualize, and hope for a future that resonates with your true self?

Future planning is akin to charting a map for a journey yet to be embarked upon. The essence lies not in predicting every twist and turn but in preparing oneself for the adventure ahead. As you stride forward in your coming out journey, may you do so with hope, conviction, and a vision that's illuminated by the brilliance of your authentic self. The future is a canvas, and your truth is the brush. Paint it beautifully.

Chapter 10: Support Systems

The narrative of our lives is not one we pen alone. Intertwined with our story are the voices, hands, and hearts of those around us - the ones who lift us when we stumble, who cheer for our triumphs, and who sit beside us in moments of reflection. This chapter, "Support Systems," shifts the lens toward these integral pillars in our journey, urging you to examine the networks, communities, and individuals that stand beside you as you traverse your coming out path.

Why spotlight "Support Systems"? Because no journey, especially one as profound and transformative as coming out, is undertaken in solitude. There's strength in unity, in shared experiences, and in the collective wisdom of those who've walked before us or alongside us. Recognizing, nurturing, and sometimes even seeking out these support structures can be pivotal to the process of self-acceptance, resilience, and growth.

Life, with its myriad challenges and celebrations, often underscores the value of a strong support system. Whether it's family, friends, professionals, or community groups, having a dependable network can be the anchor that grounds us, providing perspective, understanding, and encouragement.

The following questions are crafted to help you evaluate, appreciate, and possibly expand your support system. They are gateways to introspection about the people and platforms you lean on, and how they might evolve as your journey unfolds. Reflect on the following anchors of support:

1. Do you currently have individuals in your life who you believe will stand by you unconditionally during your coming out journey?
2. Have you reached out to or considered joining local or online LGBTQ+ support groups or communities?
3. Are there mentors or guides, perhaps those who've experienced a similar journey, that you can turn to for wisdom and advice?
4. Do you feel the need for professional support, such as counselors or therapists, specializing in LGBTQ+ issues?
5. Have you communicated your feelings and needs to your close ones, ensuring they understand the kind of support you seek?
6. Are there places or safe spaces where you feel validated, accepted, and understood?
7. Do you believe there's value in periodically evaluating and adapting your support systems to align with your evolving journey?
8. Have you thought about how you might reciprocate and become a pillar of support for others in their journeys?
9. Are there books, podcasts, or other resources that have been instrumental in offering support and perspective?
10. Do you recognize the importance of sometimes seeking solitude and self-reflection as a form of support?

Support systems are the tapestry that envelopes us, crafted from threads of empathy, understanding, and shared experience. As you navigate your coming out journey, may you find solace in the strength of these bonds, drawing from them the courage to be your most authentic self. Remember, while the path you tread is uniquely yours, the footprints of support beside you amplify its significance and beauty.

What Is Your Result?

How many Yes or No answers do you have?

Yes =

No =

Are You Ready To Coming Out?

What are your thoughts?

Conclusion

As we reach the final pages of this journey together, I'd like to pause for a moment to extend my heartfelt gratitude. Thank you for choosing this book, for giving your time, and most importantly, for embarking on this introspective voyage with me. Every page turned and every question pondered signifies a step toward understanding, acceptance, and growth.

Now, here's a small request and, perhaps, one last reflection. Think of all the times you've sought guidance or clarity and turned to books for solace, insights, or simply a nudge in the right direction. Recollect how you felt when you stumbled upon a gem, driven there, in part, by the words of others who had traversed that path before you.

By sharing your thoughts in this book, you don't just honor our journey together, but you also light the way for countless others. Your review has the power to amplify this message, to echo its resonance, and to touch the lives of those teetering on the edge of their own discoveries.

So, if this book has touched a chord, made you reflect, or even sparked a debate within, I humbly ask that you leave a review. Your words might be the beacon that guides another soul to these pages, offering them the clarity, solace, or validation they seek.

Together, through shared stories, reflections, and insights, we create a tapestry of understanding and connection. And isn't that the most magical aspect of our shared human experience? Thank you once again for being an integral part of this narrative. Here's to many more journeys of discovery, growth, and connection.

www.ingramcontent.com/pod-product-compliance
Lightning Source LLC
Chambersburg PA
CBHW060813260726
48660CB00002B/930